iCHOOSE

Actions *and* Reactions

KIMOLA BROWN LOWE

WehYahSeh Publishing
LIFE-GIVING WORDS

Published by: **WehYahSeh Publishing**

www.wehyahsehpublishing.com

Art direction: Dale Jean Paul Lowe

ISBN: (Paperback) 978-976-96217-4-9

ISBN: (Kindle)   978-976-96217-5-6

ENDORSEMENTS

I have been challenged and inspired by Kimola's writing. As I read her work, I felt the nudging of the Holy Spirit which caused me to do some introspection. Her book challenges you to think carefully about your choices and to consider whether or not they are part of God's masterplan for your life. I am inspired and encouraged. Thank you, woman-of-God, for listening to and following the leading of the Holy Spirit. I would encourage anyone who wants to live a Holy Spirit-led life, to read this book.

Chelsea Carter-Hamilton
Editor, Educator, Examiner & Songwriter

In a time where many are addicted to distraction, it necessitates visionaries like Pastor Kimola Brown Lowe to release a product that gets people focused on what is really important. *iChoose* will provide you with a tremendous and life-transforming journey, resulting in a total metamorphosis, one decision at a time. Choose *'iChoose'* and unleash a better version of yourself, as the principles are applied.

Bishop Courtney McLean
Author, Founder & Pastor
Worship & Faith Int. Fellowship (WAFIF)

Decisions are thought-based, which usually translates into actions. Even the greatest of intentions must be made out of an issue of choice. I therefore choose and make this completely, conscious decision to endorse this enlightening book *iChoose*. It will compel its readers to ponder on the actions they take, as they will recognize their lives are based on choices.

Well done Pastor Kimola Brown-Lowe on this your debut publication. Thanks for choosing to share these revelations with the world.

Pastor Courtney Morrison
Radio Broadcaster, Lecturer & Male Advocate
Pastor, Fellowship Tabernacle (Portmore)

Contents

ACKNOWLEDGEMENTS iii

DEDICATION iv

BACKGROUND v

CONDITIONS APPLY 1

REAPERS KEEPERS 5

COUNTING.... 8

WHICH WAY? 12

SEEK GOD FIRST 16

CHOOSE TO BELIEVE GOD 19

COURAGE 22

THE MIND OF CHRIST 25

CHOOSE TO HONOUR AUTHORITY 29

CHOOSE TO LOVE 33

BELIEVING IS SEEING 36

CHOOSE TO BELIEVE 40

CHOOSE TO BE SATISFIED 42

CHOOSE WISELY 45

WHO ARE YOU? 48

SEEK GOD FOR YOUR PURPOSE 50

CHOOSE HIS WILL 54

THE RIGHT SPIRIT 57

RENEW YOUR MIND 60

RIGHTEOUS MEN NEEDED 63

KEEP GOOD COMPANY 66

CHOOSE GROWTH TO OVERCOME FEAR.........................69

PREPARATION IS KEY 73

CHOOSE STRONG LEADERSHIP 76

ASK...79

WISDOM 82

CHOOSE TO STAND OUT 85

TRANSFORMATION..88

CHOOSE TO BE HEALED 91

JESUS THE WAY...93

TAKE UP YOUR CROSS..97

I CHOOSE LYRICS..99

ABOUT THE AUTHOR 101

ACKNOWLEDGEMENTS

I would like to use this opportunity to acknowledge a few key persons who helped to see this project through. First, let me acknowledge God who has afforded me the inspiration, grace and strength to complete this devotional. I am so grateful to Maureen Hamilton for suggesting that I do this devotional. You patiently waited, gently nudged and encouraged me until it all came together. Thanks to you, I can say I am a published author. Thanks to my husband for your constant and consistent support; thanks also for the perfect cover design. You add so much value to my life. I also acknowledge my mentees of Choosers Nation Twelve. The twelve of you that God has entrusted me to mentor, have challenged me to be my best self. Thanks to my Bishop, Bishop Courtney McLean for pushing me to produce. Ansil & Chelsea Hamilton, thanks for all your support. To all of you who will purchase, read or gift this book, I feel so much gratitude in my heart for you. Thank you all.

Kimola Brown Lowe

DEDICATION

I dedicate this book to my daughter Gabrielle Lowe. You are a Chooser, my princess, so choose...

BACKGROUND

iChoose: Actions and Reactions motivational devotional series came out of the song "I Choose" from the album of the same name. _I Choose_ is also the title track of the album. The final product is nothing compared to how the song was birthed. The words for the chorus came first and then the verses followed. Unlike other songs I wrote, that flowed as I worshipped, _I Choose_ never came with a melody, only the words came. For the album, this song took me the longest to write. I have been blessed with the supernatural ability to write a song in 20 minutes maximum; however, the song _I Choose_ took me days to write. I wanted it to be relevant to every generation.

The challenge I had writing this song stretched me musically. I love reggae; I am 100% Jamaican; it is in me. So, when the beat dropped in the studio, it challenged me to think and push myself to put the lyrics melodiously to the tune. Doing this made the song very real to me; it challenged me to be a chooser.

I Choose, until now, is one of my favourites, and by far, what I believe, is one of my greatest pieces of work. My favourite lines in the song are, *"Your choices determine your action, and your action, your reaction. Some people choose to live in the realm of satisfaction, but I choose the realm of manifestation."*

In other words, what you choose will reflect in your actions, and how you act will determine how life will react to you. Remain in hunger mode; keep striving to do better. Be determined to give your whole self; inspire and pour into others until the day you die.

I Choose Album is available on iTunes and other online platforms.

I trust this ***iChoose*** motivational devotional series will bless, inspire and empower your life to make good and right choices.

CONDITIONS APPLY

**The foolishness of man
perverteth his way: and his
heart fretteth against the Lord
(Proverbs 19:3).**

*E*very choice you make, will help to build the life you will live. Whatever you are doing now will either have a positive or negative impact on your future.

**Whatever you are doing now,
will either have a positive or negative impact
on your future.**

Are you comfortable with some of the choices you are making for your life? Think about it carefully…

What impact will the choices you make now, have on your future?

To make the right choices, we must do things God's way; to achieve that, we have to get to know God and His ways. How do we know God? We know God through His word.

So, when people get angry at the Lord, it is really His word that they are angry at. I have had experiences in my life, where I read the word of God and applied it, but never really got the results I expected. The next thing that crossed my mind was that this thing does not work, despite popular beliefs.

I have since learned that God's words are principles/laws written to us - as a guide for our lives.

Science teaches us that a law is guaranteed to work, once applied under the correct conditions; now, if we deviate and the word/law/principle doesn't work, the originator is not the one at fault.

God's word must be applied under the right conditions in order to get the best results from it. If we apply the word with selfish ambitions and iniquity in our hearts, it will not work for us.

According to Psalm 138:2, God honours His word above His name, so He guarantees His word.

It is foolish to think that we can get what we want from God, doing things our own way. We will not keep our job or get promoted if we are always late for work or meeting deadlines; the same applies with the word of God. If we want the right results, we must do it His way. It would be foolish to think we can access it any way we choose. When our lives and motives line up, as our faith is lifted, then we will see the full effect of His word in our lives.

I choose to live by God's design; what do you choose?

____

____

What areas of your life do you need to bring into alignment with God's word?

____

____

____

____

____

____

____

PRAYER

Father, today I submit my will to you. Today I step back into alignment with your word, so that it will take its full effect in my life, in Jesus' name. Amen.

REAPERS KEEPERS

Be not deceived; God is not mocked: for whatsoever a man soweth, that shall he also reap (Galatians 6:7).

Choices are like seeds; making them, is like sowing into the big garden called life.

Choices are like seeds; making them, is like sowing into the big garden called life.

Some of the decisions we make in life, the results can only be rectified through the power of the blood of Jesus. Some of us by virtue of our decisions in the past, are now reaping a very unfortunate present.

Some of us by virtue of our decisions in the past, are now reaping a very unfortunate present.

We sometimes learn of the harsh realities of our choices, when it is too late, and at that point we are not able to control all of the consequences.

When you sow a choice, it comes back to you- multiplied.

When you sow a choice, it comes back to you multiplied. Usually, it comes back to you long after you have sown it.

This is suggesting that what you are getting now, is a result of what you have sown in the past.

We can all testify that the favour we are receiving now, we do not deserve it. But because of the love of our Father in Heaven, we receive favour. Let us stop and tell Him thanks right now.

Still, we must move forward making better decisions, so that we can be satisfied early. The more we strive to get it right, the less time it takes to get to our destiny in God.

I choose to sow good seeds and water them with God's word and prayer; what do you choose?

____

____

____

PRAYER

Lord today I surrender to your trimming, pruning, and cutting, knowing that it is working for my good. Thanks for giving me the grace to do so, in Jesus' name. Amen.

COUNTING....

***So teach us to number our days,
that we may apply our hearts
unto wisdom (Psalm 90:12).***

God gives us time and He teaches us how to use it wisely. Ephesians 5:14-16 tells us that *"Christ shall give thee light. See then that ye walk circumspectly, not as fools, but as wise, redeeming the time, because the days are evil. Wherefore be ye not unwise, but understanding what the will of the Lord is."* John 9:4 encourages us to *"...work the works of him that sent me, while it is day: the night cometh, when no man can work."*

God gives us time and season, as outlined in Ecclesiastes 3:1-8; a time for everything under the sun. Let us use our time wisely.

In Psalm 90:10, the Bible records that our life-span is on average, seventy years – *"The days of our years are threescore years and ten; and if by reason of strength they be fourscore years,"* and by reason of strength we may get to eighty. This number in days is equal to 25,550 days. If you subtract the number of days that you have lived already, then you will know how many more possible days you have left to live. (365 x 70=25,550). What we do with those days, is particularly important to you being successful in life. Are you spending your time wisely?

Success should not be weighed by financial accomplishments, but by fulfilment of purpose.

Success should not be weighed by financial accomplishments, but by fulfilment of purpose.

Every choice we make,
Brings us closer to,
Or farther away from our purpose.

Every choice we make, brings us closer to, or farther away from our purpose. It is important to note that time lost, cannot be regained; therefore, we must pay attention to what we choose to do with our time.

Choose to invest your time wisely by prioritizing. Let nothing take the place of what is first, like your relationship with the Lord, your family, your vision, mission, and purpose. With so many distractions in the world today, it's your choices that will determine your success.

I choose to make better use of my time; what do you choose?

____

____

____

PRAYER

Lord, please help me to make better choices of how to use my time. I understand that what I do with my time will affect my life now and later. So please help me to use my time wisely. Please grant me grace in this area of my life, in Jesus' name. Amen.

WHICH WAY?

*Jesus saith unto him, I am the way, the truth, and the life: no man cometh unto the Father, but by me. (**John** 14:6)*

L
ife sometimes comes down to two choices.

However, when you are in a position in life where the bad is what sustains you, it is hard to choose the good. There are people who are trapped in situations that forces them to choose what goes against God's word. And though they know that what they are doing is wrong, what is more important to them is their survival.

The Bible reminds us in Matthew 7:1-3 that the broad road leads to destruction, but the narrow road leads to eternal life. Many people find it difficult to live life being restricted from certain things. They try to find joy in the perishable things in life: money, sex, drugs, houses, vehicles....

However, joy does not come from these things, but from God. Jesus reminds us in Matthew 6:24 *"no man can serve two masters."* In the same way we cannot be bad and be good at the same time; one will override the other; and bad tends to stand out a lot more than the good, as in the case of King Uzziah who did many great things in Israel, yet the people only remembered him having leprosy. One bad choice can ruin your life, if you allow it to. Bad seeds sometimes grow the biggest trees in the garden of life.

One bad choice can ruin your life, if you allow it to. Bad seeds sometimes grow the biggest trees in the garden of life.

It is so easy to mess up, but the remedy for not messing up or redeeming oneself, is applying the word of God daily. Stick to the narrow path, no matter how enticing the other side looks, as pointed out in Proverbs 14:11-12 - *"The house of the wicked shall be overthrown: but the tabernacle of the upright shall flourish. There is a way which seemeth right unto a man, but the end thereof are the ways of death.*

God is so gracious, He gives us the answers to life's issues upfront; Deuteronomy 30:15-19, *"See, I have set before you today life and good, death and evil…I command you today to love the LORD your God, to walk in His ways, I call heaven and earth as witnesses today against you, that I have set before you life and death, blessing and cursing; therefore choose life, that both you and your descendants may live…"*

The options are clearly outlined above. Which way will you choose?

____

____

____

PRAYER

Lord I am at a crossroad in my life, and I need your help. Please give me the courage to make the right choices, in Jesus' name. Amen.

SEEK GOD FIRST

But seek ye first the kingdom of God, and his righteousness; and all these things shall be added unto you (Matthew 6:33).

We all have a list of things we are seeking in our lives. The list may change with age and exposure. The more that is added to our lives, the greater the responsibility and the more our priorities change.

However, Jesus is telling us that our list should flow in this order, the Kingdom of God, His righteousness and then everything else after. When we seek God for the intangibles like love, faith and courage, the tangible will automatically attach itself. Once we have this order established, then we are on our way to success.

We can get so busy in everyday life, seeking the tangible things, that we lose our sense of God. When things become the centre of our lives, we can find ourselves doing whatever it takes to attain them.

We must choose to put God first in all things and by this, I mean, first doing what pleases and lines up with His word and will for our lives.

It is easy to put things before the Kingdom because the intangibles cannot be touched, so they offer less comfort than having things.

But things can crash, mash or burn, while investments such as love, pay out much higher returns. When things take the place of God, they become idols in our lives.

I choose God's Kingdom above the things of the world. What do you choose?

____

____

PRAYER

Lord today I choose to step back into alignment with seeking your Kingdom and righteousness. I repent of idolatry and ask you to forgive me for not putting you first in my life, in Jesus' name. Amen.

CHOOSE TO BELIEVE GOD

And Moses lifted up his hand, and with his rod he smote the rock twice: and the water came out abundantly, and the congregation drank...And the Lord spake unto Moses and Aaron, Because ye believed me not, to sanctify me in the eyes of the children of Israel, therefore ye shall not bring this congregation into the land which I have given them (Numbers 20:11-12).

One moment of doubt can cost you an inheritance, which took a lifetime of hard work and heartbreaks to achieve. Moses was angry at the children of Israel and disobeyed God, and for that he lost his opportunity to see The Promised Land. God carefully assessed the root of Moses' reaction and not just his actual reaction. What Moses lacked was complete trust in God. Moses did what he knew would bring immediate results because of the pressure he came under, from the children of Israel. It is a strong possibility that in that moment, anything Moses did to the rock, it would have responded; but God did not get the glory out of it, because it was not done His way.

What you are doing might be yielding the results you want, from even a tough place; but, is it how God wants you to get the results?

> **What you are doing now might be yielding the results you want, even from a tough place;**
> **BUT,**
> **is it how God wants you to get the results?**

God has your best interest at heart, in all He tells you to do. What He says sometimes does not make much sense, based on natural laws, but His wisdom supersedes all others. God trusted Moses with raw power, and Moses' ability to still trust God above the noise was important to God. When God allows us to walk in power, we must be careful, that we do not choose to impress others, or succumb to pressure from people and end up losing our greater reward.

> **When God allows us to walk in power, we must be careful that we do not choose to impress others, or succumb to pressure from people and end up losing our greater reward.**

Make the choice to listen to God, despite what people around you are saying. Think for yourself and keep your focus on Jesus.

I choose to believe God; who do you choose to believe?

PRAYER

Lord help us to have the courage to believe and obey you despite the noise around us, in Jesus' name. Amen.

COURAGE

And he said, Come. And when Peter was come down out of the ship, he walked on the water, to go to Jesus. (Matthew 14:29).

It takes much courage to do something that you know has never been done before. But no one became great playing it safe. Every great person took a risk. Once you make the choice to step out, there are a few consequences you must deal with.

Firstly, those who you left behind, may become back-biters. Secondly, if there is any sign of doubt in your mind, that risk has the potential to drown you.

However, one thing you can be sure of, is that once you are heading in the same direction with Jesus, He will pick you up if you fall. Peter stepping out of the boat, is like buying a house in a bad market or opening a business in a recession. But if you want to make the history books, you cannot make it sitting in what makes you feel safe.

You have to step out; and sometimes what you are stepping out on, was not even built to carry you. Once whatever you are going to do, is approved by Jesus, then step with all confidence, knowing that things that are not made to carry you, will have to adjust.

> **Once whatever you are going to do, is approved by Jesus, then step with all confidence, knowing that things that are not made to carry you, will have to adjust.**

I choose to be more courageous and trust God to take me through. What do you choose to do?

____

____

____

In what areas of your life have you been procrastinating? Make some bold steps now and tackle what you have been putting off.

____

____

____

____

____

____

____

____

PRAYER

Lord, today I boldly step out on your Word, trusting you to carry me to my destiny. I will not take my eyes off you and I will not be afraid. Help me to trust you, in Jesus' name. Amen.

THE MIND OF CHRIST

Casting down imaginations, and every high thing that exalteth itself against the knowledge of God, and bringing into captivity every thought to the obedience of Christ; (2 Corinthians 10:5).

Be a chooser. If you do not choose, someone else or something else will choose for you.

**Be a chooser.
If you do not choose –
someone else or something else
will choose for you.**

Many persons have made what they thought was the right choice, but what they chose, brought them their deepest regret.

Do not shelve your dreams because you had a few bad experiences. Read the biography of many successful persons today; you will see that they failed many times before they succeeded. Failure is not to break you; failure is an opportunity to learn.

> **Do not shelve your dreams because you had a few bad experiences - failure is not to break you: it is an opportunity to learn.**

How you perceive what is happening, is essential to the outcome. Choose your responses wisely. You are not the originator of every thought. Some thoughts are a direct assignment from hell, and they are sometimes subtle thoughts.

We must remember when we wrestle with ungodly thoughts and we feel like we fail, and face our hardest trials, that God still has a plan for our lives; we must continue to seek Him to know His mind, through His word. The more you study God's word, His thoughts become your thoughts, and you will realize you are becoming more like Him for *"we have the mind of Christ."*

Therefore, let God's word guide your thoughts. It is imperative that we know God's word so that we are able to cast down the imaginations - thoughts that exalt themselves against the knowledge of God (2 Corinthians 10:5). Do not allow thoughts to govern your life; but rather, choose to govern your thoughts with God's word.

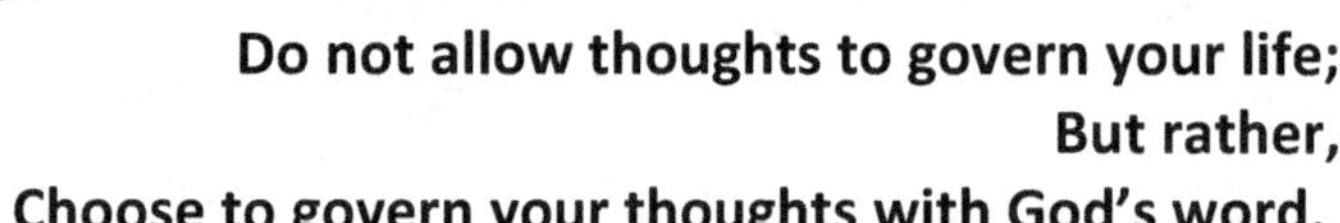

Do not allow thoughts to govern your life;
But rather,
Choose to govern your thoughts with God's word.

I choose to study God's word to know His mind and govern my thoughts; what do you choose?

____

____

PRAYER

Lord, today by your mighty power, I cast down every thought that exalts itself against your knowledge. I declare that I have power over thoughts. I declare that my thoughts are your thoughts. In Jesus' name, amen.

CHOOSE TO HONOUR AUTHORITY

***Submit yourselves to every ordinance of man for the Lord's sake: whether it be to the king, as supreme* (1 *Peter* 2:13).**

It is the norm for people to speak out against government, simply because it is easier to be critical when you are not in the position.

Though some of the decisions that our government leaders sometimes make, which may seem like they did not think about the people when making them, we still have the responsibility to honour our governmental leaders.

When we speak negativity against them, we spread and support a culture of disorder. We may not agree with everything that is decided by the government, but the scripture instructs us to submit ourselves; though we will not go against our belief in doing something that negates what the Heavenly Constitution teaches.

However, what we should do, is pray, and show respect, so that the next generation will learn by example. This does not rule out peaceful protest, but it does emphasize exercising our rights within the permitted scope of the law.

The scripture mentioned is also encouraging us to pay our taxes, obey the traffic regulations and do what is required of us as citizens of whichever country we reside in or visit.

Our enemy is not the state. What we ought to do as God's people, is to encourage godly principles and play our part as the branch of government that is responsible for moral guidance, and maintenance of the honour and reverence for the Creator.

When we get involved in the areas we are not supposed to, and get corrupted, then it reflects badly on the church. We have a choice, either to make the situation worse or to be the catalyst, pioneering change in our society.

Today I commit to praying for our government and leaders and volunteering to uplift my *community* in every way I can; what do you choose to do?

How can you show more honour to authority in different areas of your life? (Home, school, work, community, church, etc.).

____

____

____

____

____

____

____

____

____

____

PRAYER

Father, today I pray for our nation and all our leaders in every sector. Please lead and guide them daily and help them to follow the principles you outlined in your word. I pray that you will give us the strength we need to fully obey your word. Cause us to understand what you are saying to us through your words, so that we can be in right standing with you. We depend on your sufficient grace and Holy Spirit to lead us daily and we choose to honour you in all we say and do, in Jesus' name. Amen.

CHOOSE TO LOVE

***Not rendering evil for evil, or
railing for railing: but
contrariwise blessing; knowing
that ye are thereunto called,
that ye should inherit a blessing
(1 Peter 3:9).***

One of the most challenging things to do, is to love someone who shows you hate. When people rise up against you and your family, it is not always the easiest thing to show them love. What comes naturally, is to return the same measure of treatment issued out to you.

Anger and retaliation are *natural* reactions to insults. Blessing someone who does evil to you, is not the first thing on anyone's mind. But this is what God requires of us. What causes most people to retaliate is the fear of being seen as weak or as a person everyone can walk over.

When you make the choice to walk away, you are also making the choice to look like a coward. But, when you understand that feuding leads to nowhere, you see the need to let people think what they want to.

Showing love in hurtful situations, comes through the power of the Holy Spirit working in us. The Apostle Paul encourages us to be filled with the Spirit. A choice like this is not emotional, it is pure willpower. We must submit our will to the Holy Spirit to function properly. Proverbs 15:1 reminds us that a soft answer turns away wrath. Giving a soft answer is an act of humility and love.

Many people lose their lives by retaliating or taking revenge. When you are upset, you are not thinking through what you are doing, and you sometimes end up doing things you later regret and are not able to rectify.

Don't just think about winning in that moment, think about winning long-term.

Today I choose and make every effort to act in love; what do you choose?

How can you show more love to others? Will you choose to forgive your offenders? What situation(s) can you remedy today?

____

____

____

____

____

____

____

____

PRAYER

Father, today I pray that you take control of my will and emotions. Help me to restrain myself from repaying evil with evil; let my response be to love - choosing to love, in Jesus' name. Amen.

BELIEVING IS SEEING

***And Elijah came unto all the people, and said, How long halt ye between two opinions? if the LORD be God, follow him: but if Baal, then follow him. And the people answered him not a word** (1 **Kings** 18:21).*

Often, we find ourselves halting between two opinions. The longer we waver, the harder it is for us to make a decision. Especially when it comes to making life-changing decisions, it is very tedious because one of the choices always seems more readily redeemable than the other.

There is a saying that is ingrained in human culture, which says "seeing is believing." This statement is used to govern many people in the world, because every other person you meet, struggles with some kind of insecurity, maybe because of past experiences or just fear.

When you look at Baal versus God, you are looking at tangible versus intangible. In other words, because I can see it, makes it more believable. When people are caught in a situation like this, a person who has never proven either God or Baal will lean more towards what they can see, because it brings more security. This is the same reason, why people would choose a man, a job an addiction or even a religion over believing in the God they cannot see, because people will believe more in what they can see.

Even today, people are more interested and get excited over tangible things like houses, vehicles, etc., but they fail to celebrate really important intangibles such as deliverance and healing.

If you are looking for a fleshly connection with God, it is not possible, because the Bible tells us in John 4:24 that *"God is a*

Spirit: and they that worship him must worship him in Spirit and in truth." Our relationship with God is a spiritual one. To connect with God, you must connect to Him in Spirit.

Even when choosing other things in life, we have to use our spiritual eyes, and look beyond what meets the natural eyes and see potential: **believe** to **see**.

> **We have to look beyond what meets the natural eyes and see potential: Believe to see.**

Are you willing to take God at His word and believe what He says about you? Note some of what His word says about you.

____

____

____

____

____

____

What are you believing God to see? Write your vision, trust God, and pursue it.

____
____
____
____
____
____
____
____
____
____
____
____
____
____

PRAYER

Father, today give us the strength to see beyond the natural. Help us to know that though we cannot see you, we can trust you. Strengthen our faith in you, in Jesus' name. Amen.

CHOOSE TO BELIEVE

Jesus said unto him, If thou canst believe, all things are possible to him that believeth (Mark 9:23).

Faith is the key to accessing what God has for us. When we exercise our faith, we please God. Nothing is limited to us when we walk in faith. Faith has an attitude. It is not doubtful and does not get weary. Faith knows how to wait.

**Faith has an attitude.
It is not doubtful and does not get weary.
Faith knows how to wait.**

When we put our trust in God, we have to believe that he is faithful and just to answer us.

Prayer without faith is merely a ritual, but when we apply faith, we get results. A faithless church is a stagnant church. A church that has faith, will carry God's glory in the earth. We should not have partial faith where we are only able to believe God for small things. We should stretch ourselves to believe God for anything and everything. If we can believe God for it, we can access it. Let us activate our faith today.

Will you trust and believe God no matter what? What are you trusting God for?

____

____

PRAYER

Dear God, we ask you give us the grace to believe not just for the small things, but for the big things. We ask that you touch our minds, so that we will not limit you by the disappointments we have faced in our lives. Help us to appreciate your love for us and give us grace to always trust you, in Jesus' name. Amen.

CHOOSE TO BE SATISFIED

**Envy thou not the oppressor,
and choose none of his ways
(Proverbs 3:31).**

Crime and violence are very lucrative business practices in many parts of the world. Many people get involved in crime and violence for the same reason; whether they are rich or poor, being unsatisfied is the cause.

Some people always want more, no matter how much they already have. So, they do illegitimate things to gain more. Many times, you see them prospering in their unlawfulness and you start to equate your life to theirs.

However, the end of a man who lives like this, is destruction. The Apostle Paul wrote in Philippians 4:11, *"Not that I speak in respect of want: for I have learned, in whatsoever state I am, therewith to be content."* I am not saying that you should not desire great things for your life, you should; but not to the point where you would do anything illegal to attain them.

Choose satisfaction; do not be like the violent man, for they go after what they do not have at any cost. Violent people are arrogant and prideful, and they commit acts of violence because they lack humility.

Humility is the foundation of every great leader. Do not be envious because of what people have, *"But my God will supply all your need..."* (Philippians 4:19).

I choose to be satisfied; are you satisfied?

Do you find yourself in questionable situations that do not line up with God's word? What do you choose to do about it?

____

____

____

PRAYER

Father, I trust you. I know that whatever you are doing in my life will work together for my good, so I trust you to order my steps. I lift my faith to you, and I believe your word. Today, I choose to be thankful and satisfied. Amen.

CHOOSE WISELY

Receive my instruction, and not silver; and knowledge rather than choice gold (Proverbs 8:10).

When you put wealth and riches in competition with instructions and knowledge, it is not hard to deny the latter, especially when you are in need.

Your mind must be renewed in order to see the importance of instructions and knowledge over wealth and riches. One must realize that once you know how to do it, and you have the guidance to help you get it done, wealth and riches will not be an issue.

However, that is not the first thing people think about when they are in distress. What you must therefore realize, is that, without knowledge and instructions, wealth and riches can quickly and easily disappear; you can lose it much faster than you came by it. So, choose wisely where this is concerned.

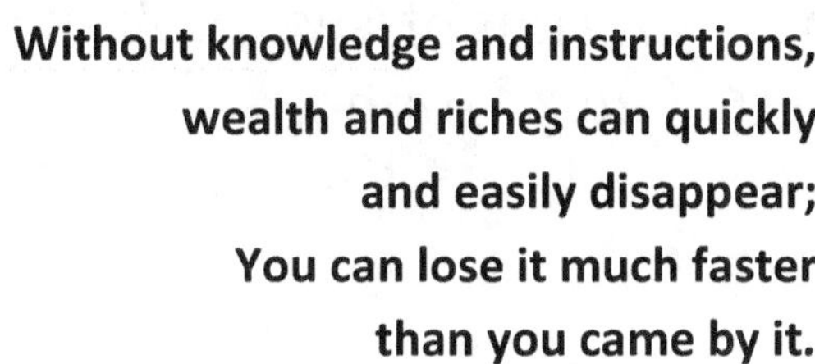

Are you making wise and smart financial and other choices for today and your future? What decisions do you need to take now to make better and wiser choices going forward?

____

____

____

____

____

____

PRAYER

Father, the desire for wealth sometimes outweighs the search for truth. Many times, because of how I was socialised, I cannot see the value in knowledge and instructions from you. Lead me into all truth, so I might see your blessed way, in Jesus' name. Amen.

WHO ARE YOU?

*But ye are a chosen generation,
a royal priesthood, an holy
nation, a peculiar people; that
ye should shew forth the praises
of him who hath called you out
of darkness into his marvellous
light: (1 Peter 2:9).*

Sometimes we lose a sense of who we are, and God has no issue in reminding and reassuring us. Most of the times when He does it, it is at a time when we are not behaving in a manner that represents what He is saying about us; yet, He does it anyway.

He chose us, and when He chooses something or someone, He does not change His mind about them despite that person's behaviour. Even when we do not qualify for what he has chosen us for, He qualifies us and sticks with us, until we get it right. God does not make a choice and then leaves it; He stands by it.

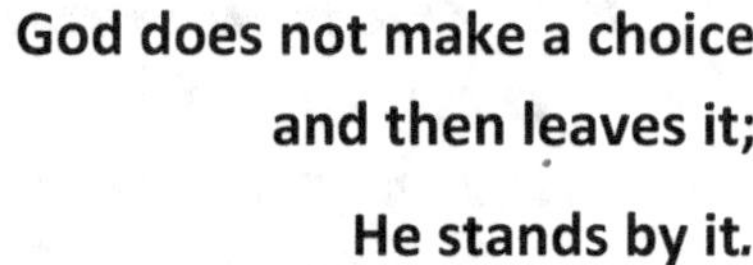

I am grateful today that God does not turn His back on us. Even when we fail, He is there to help us pick up the broken pieces. Through His word, He reminds us of who we are: chosen. God is amazing, and He truly loves us.

Remind yourself of what God thinks about you.

____

____

____

PRAYER
Father, thank you for loving us and never giving up on us, though we have failed you many times. I love you Lord. Amen.

SEEK GOD FOR YOUR PURPOSE

**Before I formed thee in the belly
I knew thee; and before thou
camest forth out of the womb I
sanctified thee, and I ordained
thee a prophet unto the nations
(Jeremiah 1:5).**

What I like most about God is that He is not indecisive. He is not confused about what He is doing; He knows what He wants done in the earth and He knows who is best to perceive, release, and cultivate it.

God does not second-guess when He creates. He knew from the beginning why and how He wanted you to be formed. He even knows what He thinks towards you. Being the God that He is - Alpha and Omega, He already knows your end, from your beginning. So, if we are created in His image and likeness, uncertainty is not one of His traits; it is not in His DNA. Why then are we so unsure about our destiny and purpose? At times we make the wrong choices and end up in terrible situations. What are we missing?

Jesus encourages us in Matthew 6:33 to seek first the Kingdom. When we seek the Kingdom, automatically we seek the King.

When we are in the presence of the King, he will speak to us and show us His plans for us; our power is in our choices...

> When we are in the presence of the King,
> He will speak to us
> and show us His plans for us;
> our power is in our choices.

We can either choose to obey or forsake the King. The choice is yours; choose wisely. We sometimes lose out on our purpose because we choose not to submit to the King.

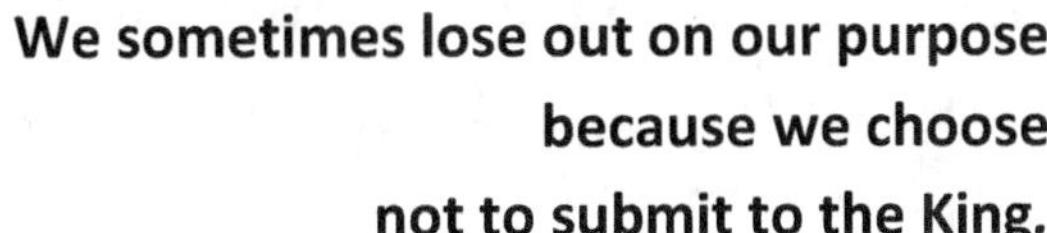

**We sometimes lose out on our purpose
because we choose
not to submit to the King.**

Sometimes our own interest and liking get the best of us, and we miss out on our divine assignment. Let us go back to the originator and find out what was his initial intention for us, so that His will and our purpose might be fulfilled.

Do you know God's purpose for your life? A good place to start is to write down a few things about yourself that come naturally to you, and you are passionate about; pursue them.

____

____

____

____

____

____

PRAYER

Father, today I am coming back to you, so that this uncertainty and lack of direction will go away, and I will know what your will is for me. Thank you for showing me your way and your purpose for my life, in Jesus' name. Amen.

CHOOSE HIS WILL

Saying, Father, if thou be willing, remove this cup from me: nevertheless not my will, but thine, be done (Luke 22:42).

According to Merriam-Webster's dictionary, the will *"is used to express desire, choice, willingness, consent, or in negative construction."*

Each day we are faced with decisions and we must use our will to make an ultimate choice. The emotions feel it, your mind thinks it, but your will acts on it.

Jesus was in the garden of Gethsemane praying about the choice God made for Him. Jesus wanted to do His Father's will and He was totally submitted to His Father. Jesus knew the main purpose why God had sent Him.

Your feelings or thoughts will not shift God's plan for your life, no matter what the circumstances. Once we know His heart towards us, then we know whatever we are facing in our lives, it is for a greater cause.

> **Your feelings or thoughts will not shift God's plan for your life, no matter what the circumstances.**

Jesus had to die because He could not save mankind unless He died.

Every hard thing we face in our life, can be used for a greater cause, if we allow God to work it out for our good. Sometimes we want to shy away from it, but because we know that the God we serve will not cause us to go through anything that is fruitless, we can trust Him to take us to it and through it. If you go through the fire, you will come out as pure gold. The fire may burn, but the end product is worth whatever you had to go through.

Therefore, when you are faced with challenges, know that God is at the end of it, waiting to receive you. So, you can trust His will because it is for you to prosper. The evidence is in 3 John 1:2 *"Beloved, I wish above all things that thou mayest prosper and be in health, even as thy soul prospereth."*

Even though I may not always understand the process, I choose to submit to His will; what do you choose?

____

____

____

____

PRAYER
Father, I thank you today, that you think good thoughts towards me. Today, I shake off the fear that you will abandon me, and I will press through, knowing that, according to your word, you are a rewarder of those who seek you; I choose your will for my life, in Jesus' name. Amen.

THE RIGHT SPIRIT

Light is sown for the righteous, and gladness for the upright in heart (Psalm 97:11).

David in Psalm 5:10 prayed, "*Create in me a clean heart, O God; and renew a right spirit within me.*" A right spirit has to be cultivated. According to Romans 10:17 "*...faith cometh by hearing...*" This suggests repetition builds faith and habit.

Therefore, constantly doing or repeating the same things, whether good or bad habits, will train and renew your mind.

Proverbs 4:23 says that out of your heart/subconscious mind, flows the issues/boundaries of life. In other words, how you react to life's situations, is an outward show of what is in your heart.

**How you react to life's situations,
is an outward show
of what is in your heart.**

Therefore, it is very important to cultivate a right spirit and renew your mind daily to get rid of anything that, left unchecked, can corrupt our heart and foster hurt, hatred and unforgiveness.

We are cautioned in Ephesians 6:26 *"...let not the sun go down upon your wrath..."* It means daily cleansing is important for the health of our heart and to maintain a right spirit.

When you store hatred, unforgiveness, and bitterness in your heart, you will not experience an abundance of joy. 2 Corinthians 6:14, confirms you cannot, because both good and bad, darkness and light cannot reign in the same vessel; one will overpower the other.

There are people who do not have joy; one of the reasons for this is because the condition of their heart is not right. Whatever is stored there, is going to flow.

As right equates to joy; so wrong equates to misery, sadness, and depression. Ask Jesus, like David in Psalms 51, to fill you with the Holy Spirit so that a right spirit can be renewed in you.

I choose to cultivate a right spirit; what do you choose?

____

____

____

____

PRAYER

Dear Father, today I want to experience the fullness of your joy. I ask you to renew a right spirit within me, so that my joy might be full. Thank you for hearing and answering my prayers, in Jesus' name. Amen.

RENEW YOUR MIND

The rich man's wealth is his strong city: the destruction of the poor is their poverty (Proverbs 10 vs 15).

And be not conformed to this world: but be ye transformed by the renewing of your mind (Romans 12:2)

Whatever your status is in life, Jesus is still relevant. Some people believe that only the poor need God, but the rich also need a Saviour. It is one thing to be rich, but it's another thing to be healthy and happy. Money cannot give you peace, as this only comes from God. No matter what we do, or do not have, we all have an area in our lives that require supernatural intervention from time to time.

Poverty is not the lack of money. You can have money and still be poor; it is how you handle and view money that makes the difference. The chorus of a song I wrote years ago says *"What a man thinketh so is he, so if you wanna walk into your destiny and be everything that you can be, you better change your mind."*

Romans 12:2 gives us the perfect antidote for any kind of poverty: mind renewal. When your mind is renewed, you will see that there is more wealth in what people consider to be the simpler things in life, like a family that loves you and good health to enjoy what you have.

When your mind is renewed, you will see that there is more wealth in what people consider to be the simpler things in life.

How you view life determines how you will live it. Blind Bartimaeus in Mark 10 was a beggar because he was blind. But when he got an opportunity to choose between a day's meal or his sight, he chose what money could not buy. There are people who are comfortable where they are, because they are being carried by someone else.

However, you must realize that your state is not determined by your physical location, but it is determined by the state of your mind. What do you choose today?

Do you choose earthly things that dim and lose their value quickly, or do you choose what money cannot buy?

When you have a renewed mind, you can gain wealth and keep it. Think on these things...

____
____
____

PRAYER
Father, I ask you today to renew my mind. Please reveal the blind spots in my life and shift my paradigm so that I will know that your name is my fortress and nothing I can ever have in this life, can give me what you can. I receive joy and peace today from your presence, in Jesus' name. Amen.

RIGHTEOUS MEN NEEDED

The name of the LORD is a strong tower; the righteous run to it and are safe (Proverbs 18:10).

Whenever God needed someone to bring change in the earth, God looked for a righteous man. Jesus looks for a man who has his priorities in order; a man of discipline and one who has good work attributes who will stick to the plan that he is given.

God then takes that man, makes him holy and separates him from all other gods. He takes away his desire for sin; this is what God did with Abraham. Being righteous therefore denotes having integrity with time, money and people. It also means being disciplined and hardworking. Being holy takes on a separate meaning. When something or someone is made holy, they are made holy as unto God.

Therefore, it means there are no competing factors for divine directives in one's life. The very first command God gave in Exodus 20:3 is that you should have no other gods beside Him; then God went on to list nine other things that should not be practiced. God needs righteous people to carry out his glory in every sector of the world.

Even persons who have the right approach to life are not safe, and the faster they realize this, the better they will be. Rich people are not without lack, and one of those areas in which they experience lack is often in the area of protection.

The truth is that people fear for their lives and so you will often find them seeking protection from sources such as astrology and other practices that can offer them a sense of security.

But for those who find Jesus, know that there is power in that name. There are many people who are just imposters who only use the name of Jesus, but they have not committed to the culture which produces that benefit.

When you put away all other gods and start to communicate with the true and living God, then you will get full coverage when you call His name. You may have all the details to doing life *right*, but the missing detail is - a safe place, and you can find that in Jesus.

I choose Jesus and His righteousness; what do you choose?

____

____

____

PRAYER

Jesus, I surrender my life to you. I need protection, and I understand what I must do, and choose to receive that now. I look to you for strength so that I can fulfil your plans and purposes for my life, in Jesus' name. I thank you. Amen.

KEEP GOOD COMPANY

And Moses said unto Joshua, Choose us out men, and go out, fight with Amalek: tomorrow I will stand on the top of the hill with the rod of God in mine hand (Exodus 17:9).

We should take the time to know those who God has placed around us, because at some point in our lives, we will need them. We should also take the time to prepare, as God can promote us at any time.

When God elevates you, will the people around you trust you enough, to go out and fight with you? Not everyone around us will appreciate us, but they must be able to respect us. Do not wait until you are promoted to earn the trust of persons through integrity and accountability.

Always be upright in your ways; you never know when you will be called on to lead the pack. Joshua had to obey Moses' command to choose some men to fight with him. Joshua had to move with agility, which means he was investing time in the people around him. If Joshua was not an honourable man, no one would have trusted him enough to lay their lives down.

When God elevates you, will the people around you trust you enough, to go out and fight with you?

Always remember that it is not only your educational status or wealth that takes you through life, but it is your ability to deal with people around you. The time will come in your life when you will have your own enemy to fight. That moment when you are not hiding behind Moses, but you are facing those enemies by yourself, you cannot go it alone; you need help.

Many of us tend to take on our trials by ourselves, but Moses gave Joshua excellent advice and that is, do not go alone, take some men with you. Do not try to attack everything on your own. Paul said in Romans 12:18 that if it is possible, live peaceably with everyone; as we say in Jamaica *mek wih liv gud*. This way, when you need back-up, someone will be there for you in times of distress.

I am choosing my company carefully; what choices are you making to reinforce your circle and live peaceably?

____

____

____

____

____

PRAYER

Father help me to live upright and just, so that in my time of distress I will have people to encourage and pray for me, in Jesus' name. Amen.

CHOOSE GROWTH TO OVERCOME FEAR

Then he which had received the one talent came and said, Lord, I knew thee that thou art an hard man, reaping where thou hast not sown, and gathering where thou hast not strawed: And I was afraid, and went and hid thy talent in the earth: lo, there thou hast that is thine. His lord answered and said unto him, Thou wicked and slothful servant, thou knewest that I reap where I sowed not, and gather where I have not strawed: Thou oughtest therefore to have put my money to the exchangers, and then at my coming I should have received mine own with usury (Matthew 25:24-27,).

God is an investor. He invests in us and He expects us to bring a return on his investment. God provides everything we need for life: trees, dirt, water, chemical particles, etc. He gives us the raw material and then He gives us the wisdom and vision of how to harvest what He has given.

God gives us the raw material and then He gives us the wisdom and vision of how to harvest what He has given.

How we view the situation that we find ourselves in, will determine what we make of it. One could say the man with one bag of gold was treated unfairly, as against the others.

However, this man seemingly had a track record based on the latter part of verse 15 in Matthew 25. It says that the talents were given according to each man's ability.

Therefore, this means that the master had done his assessment and made the distribution based on his findings. Everyone must work towards growing their abilities and producing in order to achieve more.

**Everyone must work towards growing
their abilities and producing
in order to achieve more.**

God's word says in 1 Corinthians 10:14 that God will not allow you to be tempted beyond what you can manage. Therefore, God will not make you a steward over what you cannot control. You must grow and increase in capability.

Two other observations that can be made from Matthew 25, is that the man was afraid. Fear is debilitating to your potential. The other thing is that he hid the gold in the ground; in other words, he put it in the wrong environment.

Do not allow fear to cripple you. Fear will cause you to put your gift into the wrong environment.

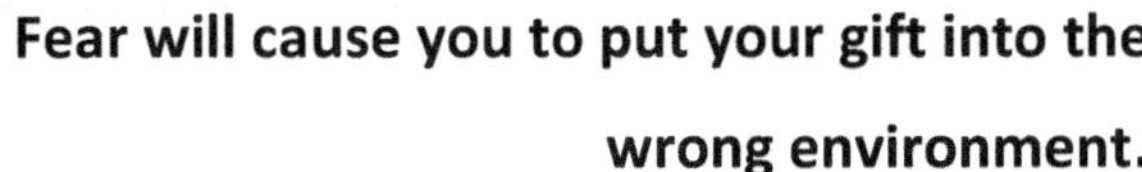

Fear will cause you to put your gift into the wrong environment.

What fears are keeping you bound? What choices can you make to better overcome those fears?

____

____

____

____

____

PRAYER

Lord today I repent for allowing fear to debilitate me and cause me to deny what you have given me. I put fear behind me and make a fresh commitment to work on what you have given me, in Jesus' name. Amen.

PREPARATION IS KEY

They that were foolish took their lamps, and took no oil with them: But the wise took oil in their vessels with their lamps (Matthew 25:4-5).

Comfort is only for those who know they are prepared for whatever is coming.

Comfort is only for those who know they are prepared for whatever is coming.

You cannot be at ease, until you know you have put things in order, for whatever surprises may pop up along the way.

Being close to destiny is not being in destiny. Sometimes you get to the door and still have to wait to access the door. The thing that will keep you going is having something in reserve.

Preparation is the key to accessing destiny. Do not wait until it is too late to ask the right questions. Ask from the get-go. The issue with the foolish virgins was not that they did not have the oil; but rather, they did not use the opportunity to learn from the wise.

All of us may look the same, but all of us are not the same. What separates us, is our ability to sense an opportunity and be ready for it.

Do not settle for the invitation based on your qualification. Exceed expectations through preparation. Based on the story of the wise and foolish virgins, being a virgin may have gotten you to the door, but only wisdom will get you through the door.

Do not settle for the invitation based on your qualification.

Exceed expectations through preparation.

In what ways can you exceed expectations in your sphere – at home, work, church, community...?

____

____

____

____

PRAYER

Father, today I repent. I have been unprepared for the opportunities you have presented me with. I make a fresh commitment today to choose preparation. I will prepare for what you have called me to do, and to go beyond expectations as I serve you and my fellowmen, in Jesus' name. Amen.

CHOOSE STRONG LEADERSHIP

But he said, Nay; lest while ye gather up the tares, ye root up also the wheat with them. Let both grow together until the harvest: and in the time of harvest I will say to the reapers, Gather ye together first the tares, and bind them in bundles to burn them: but gather the wheat into my barn (Matthew 13:29-30).

While you are busy doing life, bad things can happen to you by your own doing and by the hands and actions of other people. However, do not uproot, close down, stop or quit what you have worked so hard to start because things go wrong. Stay the course and finish what you have started, even with negativity around you, still go after what your good intentions were in the first place.

Whatever is being sown in and around your good works, can only cause damage if you stop to deal with it now. Some things you deal with right away, some things you wait until the time is right. It may slow down the process, but it cannot stop it.

As leaders, sometimes you have to start with the lows and climb to the highs to keep your team in the right frame of mind and good spirits. Highlight the bad things first, and like the scripture says, collect and tie. In other words, put things under control. Matthew 13: 30 says to collect the weeds and tie them in bundles to be burned. When it is time to harvest, there are some things you bundle and other things you gather.

In other words, only give care (gather) to those things that are deserving of it. Spend less time on the negatives.

Do not stop the celebration to light a fire either, keep it moving and when you are through gathering, then you burn.

In our lives, we must be mindful of what we pay attention to and give our best efforts to. Only focus on the seeds you have for those plants that have your next set of seeds for your next harvest.

I choose effective leadership; what do you choose to focus on?

____

____

____

____

____

PRAYER

Father, today I receive strategies for leadership. I download your wisdom and store it in my heart. I ask you to give me the grace to utilize them to lead even my own life, in Jesus' name. Amen.

ASK

***Ask and it will be given to you;
seek and you will find; knock
and the door will be opened to
you (Matthew 7:7).***

There are some things you ask for, other things you seek for, but then there are things that you have to knock in order to access them. Each level comes with a different level of aggression and a different level of reward.

Sometimes when we ask, we ask to ease an immediate struggle that we have. Most people make the most obvious thing, or the now thing, their priority.

Only a few people see an opportunity in delayed gratification. If you are going to ask, ask for wisdom and direction. If you are going to seek, seek for opportunities for advancement. If you're going to knock, aim for Goliath's head.

Seeking requires a lot of patience, and sometimes we find what we are truly looking for, only after we don't truly need it anymore.

Opportunities don't appear because you need them; they come, whether you need them or not; it's up to you to recognize and tap into them.

> **Opportunities do not appear
> because you need them;
> they come, whether you need them or not;
> it's up to you
> to recognize and tap into them.**

However, to attain them, sometimes you have to knock down, knock out and knock over some stuff in order that the right door may open for you. Asking gets you to the location of the door; seeking gets you to the door but knocking gets you through the door. When you get there, it's not time to ask or seek, it's time to knock. Start knocking, you're there!

What opportunities can you salvage or create based on your gifts and talents?

____

____

____

____

____

____

____

____

PRAYER

Today I declare I will employ the correct strategy in the appropriate place. I will take the shot I have been afraid to take, in Jesus' name. Amen.

WISDOM

Wisdom is the principal thing; therefore, get wisdom: and with all thy getting get understanding (Proverbs 4:7).

Wisdom is one thing we should seek to go after in our lives. We avoid many mistakes when we possess wisdom. The Cambridge dictionary defines wisdom as *the ability to use knowledge and experience to make good decisions and judgements.*

Therefore, wisdom must apply knowledge via the bridge of understanding. Many people seek knowledge but do not discover how to use that knowledge.

Wisdom must apply knowledge via the bridge of understanding.

Hence, they are overweight with information but to no effect, because they lack the ability to use what they know. Getting wisdom is imperative to your destiny. Solomon asked for wisdom, and in turn, he was the richest king that ever lived.

Many people go to school and get an education but end up not knowing how to apply the knowledge they owe hundreds of dollars for. Employers sometimes will go for someone with experience over someone with knowledge.

However, experience is not wisdom if you do not learn from it.

Therefore, wisdom, knowledge and understanding are a three-fold cord; together, they are not easily broken.

However, wisdom completes the bond.
You can get somewhere with knowledge, but you can own it with wisdom.

**Wisdom, knowledge and understanding
are a three-fold cord;
TOGETHER,
they are not easily broken.**

I choose to apply Godly wisdom in every area of my life; what do you choose?

____
____
____
____
____

PRAYER

Father, today I ask that you endow me with your wisdom so I will be able to make wise choices. Thank you, Lord. Amen.

CHOOSE TO STAND OUT

If this be so, our God whom we serve is able to deliver us from the burning fiery furnace, and he will deliver us out of your hand, O king. But if not, be it known to you, O king, that we will not serve your gods or worship the golden image that you have set up (Daniel 3:17-18).

Shadrach Meshach and Abednego were determined that they would not bow down to worship any other god than the God of Heaven who they served. Even when thrown in the furnace, the three Hebrew boys still were not shaken in their faith towards God. King Nebuchadnezzar, after looking closely, realized that God was also in the fire with these boys; they chose to standout and stand up for what they believed in.

God is looking for a generation who is not afraid of criticism, bullying and even chastisement from other people; a generation who will stand relentlessly for what is right.

If we fear the repercussions of our stance, we will never stand. Only people who have made peace with their fears, can prove the reality of Jesus in this time. Going against the usual is not common.

If we fear the repercussions of our stance, we will never stand. Only people who have made peace with their fears, can prove the reality of Jesus in this time.

However, whatever is common is usually not God's way. Sometimes God is working even in the strangest things.

Choose to stand up and stand out by exercising what you believe in, without fear.

I choose to stand out and do what God called me to do; what do you choose?

____

____

____

____

____

____

____

PRAYER

Dear God, today I present my fears to you and ask for your grace to stand up as a believer in this time. I realize my limitations and ask for your grace to overcome every challenge I will be faced with. I receive your grace now, in Jesus' name. Amen.

TRANSFORMATION

Do not be conformed to this world, but be transformed by the renewal of your mind, that by testing you may discern what is the will of God, what is good and acceptable and perfect (Romans 12:2).

In a world where there is so much chaos, voices, opinions and choices, we must fight to hold on to God's word. There is also a lot of pressure from our peers, society and the media to adapt a certain way of life.

> In a world where there is so much chaos, voices, opinions, and choices, we must fight to hold on to God's word.

Conforming happens in stages; one of the most effective ways to get someone to conform is to desensitize them. This accounts for the way in which certain modern lifestyles are injected in movies, music and even commercials. After a while, you get so used to seeing it, that it no longer bothers you. Sooner or later, you find yourself accepting agendas that are not godly.

Therefore, we have to constantly renew our minds using the word of God as our guide for what is acceptable and perfect. 1 Peter 5:8, cautions us to *"be sober, be vigilant; because your adversary the devil, as a roaring lion, walketh about, seeking whom he may devour."*

Just as conforming is a slow process through desensitization, transformation is a slow process through sensitization - by injecting the word of God into our daily lives.

Just as conforming is a slow process through desensitization, transformation is a slow process through sensitization- by injecting the word of God into our daily lives.

I choose to be transformed by God's word; what do you choose?

____

____

____

PRAYER

Dear God, thank you for your word. Thank you that your word can transform my life. Give me the grace to stay in your word until I am transformed. Guard my heart from evil and give me the grace to see the areas of my life that I have conformed to the world, so that I may repent and start my journey to transformation, in Jesus' name. Amen.

CHOOSE TO BE HEALED

Confess your faults one to another, and pray one for another, that ye may be healed. The effectual fervent prayer of a righteous man availeth much (James 5:16).

Sometimes, our prayers are not answered because of the posture of our hearts. We can find ourselves in a position where we have unforgiveness, resentment and offense in our hearts towards someone and this is a major hindrance to our prayers.

James encourages us in the scripture to come clean. When we free our hearts of what we have done or what we are feeling, then we are able to be healed and get answers to our prayers. We must come before the Lord clean.

Otherwise, we can stand in the way of our prayers being answered. As we ask God to forgive us, we should also forgive others.

Praying from a place of healing yields answers to our prayers. When we do what is required, like confessing our sins to one another, then we are exercising righteousness and righteousness makes our prayers effective. It is written in James 5:16 that we should *"Confess your faults one to another, and pray one for another, that ye may be healed. The effectual fervent prayer of a righteous man availeth much."*

I choose healing; what do you choose?

____

____

PRAYER
Dear God, please give us the grace for confession unto healing. In the areas we struggle to make right, expose our hearts to us Lord so that we may make the necessary adjustments in our lives, in Jesus' name. Amen.

JESUS THE WAY

Then said Jesus unto his disciples, If any man will come after me, let him deny himself, and take up his cross, and follow me (Matthew 16:24).

Jesus' statement was very conditional. The word "if" implies human action involved in the qualification process of becoming a follower. Three actions are listed in the verse: (1) deny your own way; (2) take up your cross; and (3) follow me. Let's examine each act of qualification.

First, you have to deny yourself. This means, that you will have to submit your thoughts, desires and your will to the tutelage and Lordship of Jesus. Giving up your own way is also speaking to the path you are currently on in life, in terms of your way of life. Jesus said in John 14:6 that, *"I am the way, the truth and the life."*

Giving up our way is sometimes not the easiest thing to do, because as humans, we like to do what brings us comfort. This is where the decision becomes harder to make, because following Jesus' example sometimes does not always bring comfort right away.

For example, when it comes to forgiving the people who hurt us, our way would be to get back at them. This would undoubtedly bring us satisfaction as it would be doing it our way. However, Jesus' way brings eternal life, as against our way which brings destruction.

Secondly, **take up your cross**, meaning take up your purpose. How do I know this? Jesus' ultimate purpose was to die for mankind, so when he refers to the cross, He is saying take up whatever is your cross, which is whatever you were born to do, and follow Him.

Thirdly, He said follow me. Jesus is saying here, do whatever I do, say whatever I say and go wherever I go. All of this will qualify you to become a Jesus follower, but ultimately you have to choose this path as it is not bestowed upon you.

Why should you choose this way? Because your way of doing life leads to destruction; but the simple way Jesus instructs, leads to eternal life.

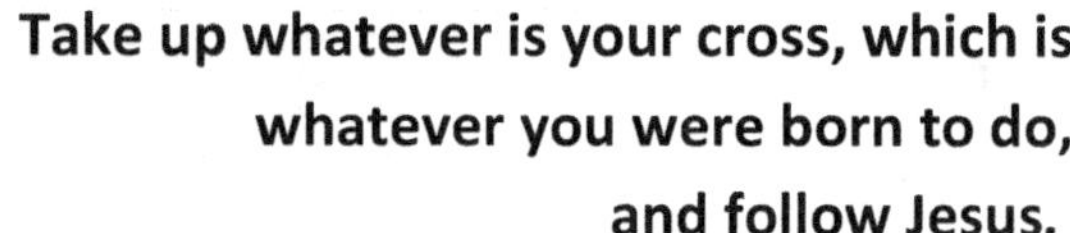

Take up whatever is your cross, which is whatever you were born to do, and follow Jesus.

What do you believe is your cross–your purpose to carry? In other words, what were you born to do?

____

____

____

____

____

____

____

____

PRAYER

Father, today I submit myself to your way. It is not always easy letting go of myself, but I choose you. Please give me the strength to follow you, in Jesus' name I pray. Amen.

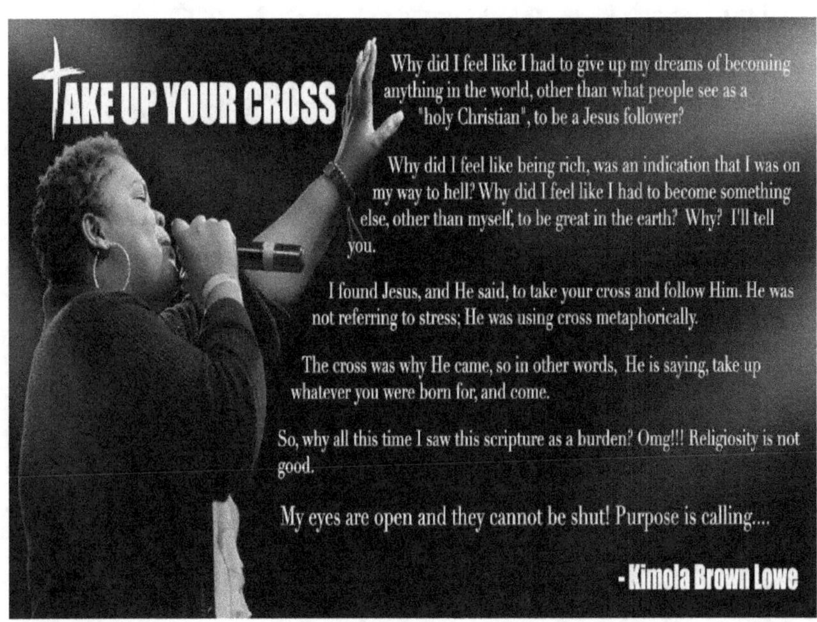

TAKE UP YOUR CROSS

Why did I feel like I had to give up my dreams of becoming anything in the world, other than what people see as a "holy Christian" to be a Jesus follower?

Why did I feel like being rich was an indication that I was on my way to hell? Why did I feel like I had to become something else other than myself to be great in the earth? Why?

I'll tell you why… religion.

I found Jesus, and He said to take up your cross and follow Him. He was not referring to stress, He was using 'cross' metaphorically.

The cross was why he came; so, in other words, He is saying, take up whatever you were born for, and come. In Matthew

16:24 *"Then said Jesus unto his disciples, If any man will come after me, let him deny himself, and take up his cross, and follow me."* The reason I saw this scripture as a burden for so long was because of *'religiosity'* ...OMG!!! The scales have been removed from my eyes; I can see clearly now.

My eyes are open, and they cannot be shut! Purpose is calling....

Kimola Brown Lowe @ January 2018

The cross was why he came;
so in other words, He is saying,
take up whatever you were born for:
take up your purpose,
and come.

Will you choose to take up your cross - your purpose and follow Jesus today?

I CHOOSE LYRICS

Chorus
I choose - I choose, His will not the benefits
I choose - I choose to live right and I'm loving it.
I choose - I choose to love my friends and my enemies
I choose, I choose.

Verse 1
I put before you life and death - choose life.
And forsaking all the wrongs - choose right,
Some people living in the dark - choose light.
You can choose to walk by faith or sight
Or you can die in this war or fight,
Use the word and put those demons to flight
The Father gave us all the strategies
to overcome the enemy.
To say no to profanity and know that which is vanity.
To regulate humanity and keep your Christian sanity.
So, which one of the roads will you choose?

Verse 2
Your choices determine your action,
And your actions, your reaction
Some people choose the realm of satisfaction
But I choose the realm of manifestation.
Some people choose to think that I have seemed
to have lost my way,
Shut off your mind, open your ears
and listen wha me a say,
The Fada gimme di vision and me choose to obey,
Mi radical, radical, radical same way.
Harvest is ripe - laborers are few
Inna di four walls you a stay?
Take off your hat, take off your tie

Go pon de highways and byways
Go mek we seek the soul dem weh a stray dem a stray
Salvation when da chune yah a play.

<u>Bridge</u>
So much religion,
Spiritual malnutrition, fighting which one and which
Making the right decisions
To go the nations or depend on radio stations
Saying there is no room for me
But I choose, I choose to go - I choose, I choose to do
I choose to say – Lord I'll obey.

I Choose Album cover

ABOUT THE AUTHOR

KIMOLA BROWN LOWE

Kimola viewed singing as her passion; however, it quickly became evident that she was not just a singer, but a gifted speaker who is always ready to share the good news of the gospel. She is a sought-after speaker, whose speaking gift and ability to motivate, has taken her to different settings including schools, universities, corporate and social settings and churches across the world. A native of St. Ann, Jamaica, Kimola Brown Lowe, is an ordained Pastor, Evangelist at heart, motivational speaker, songwriter and award-winning gospel artiste, with two albums to her credit (Lift Him Up, vol.1&2), and *I Choose*, which gave birth to the motivational devotional - ***iChoose: Actions and Reactions.*** Kimola is married to Dale Lowe and they have two beautiful daughters Allana and Gabrielle.

Contact Kimola Brown Lowe Ministries at wehyahsehpublishing@gmail.com.